The World stage navigating international relations in the 21st century

By:
Lola Jaxongirova

© Taemeer Publications LLC
The World stage: navigating international relations in the 21st century
by: Lola Jaxongirova
Edition: August '2023
Publisher:
Taemeer Publications LLC (Michigan, USA / Hyderabad, India)

ISBN 978-93-5872-130-0

© Taemeer Publications

Book	:	*The World stage: navigating international relations in the 21st century*
Author	:	Lola Jaxongirova
Publisher	:	Taemeer Publications
Year	:	'2023
Pages	:	36
Title Design	:	*Taemeer Web Design*

Table of Content

CHAPTER 1
DIPLOMACY AND INTERNATIONAL COOPERATION
--- THE IMPORTANCE OF DIPLOMACY IN INTERNATIONAL RELATIONS AND RESOLVING CONFLICTS
--- THE ROLE OF INTERNATIONAL ORGANIZATIONS IN FACILITATING COOPERATION AMONG NATIONS

CHAPTER 2
GLOBAL CHALLENGES AND CRISES
--- GLOBAL CHALLENGES OCCURING IN THE 21ST CENTURY
AND IN-DEPTH ANALYSIS OF THESE CHALLENGES
--- INTERCONNECTIVITY OF THESE CHALLENGES AND THE NEED FOR COLLOBORATION AMONG NATIONS

CHAPTER 3
ECONOMIC GLOBALIZATION AND TRADE
--- INFLUENCE OF GLOBAL TRADE IN INTERNATIONAL RELATIONS
--- HOW WORLD TRADE ORGANIZATION IS INTERCONNECTING THE COUNTRIES
--- WORLD-TRADE ORGANIZATIONS SUCH AS AMAZON AND ALIBABA

CHAPTER 4
EMERGING OPPORTUNITIES
--- THE IMPACT OF TECHNOLOGICAL ADVANCEMENTS IN INTERNATIONAL RELATIONS

WELCOME

The world today is more interconnected than ever before with nations facing complex challenges and opportunities on the global stage. In this book we are going to delve into the intricacies of international relations and analyze the key dynamics that shape the interactions between nations in the 21st century. From the rise of emerging powers to the impact of technological advancements we will explore the factors that define our modern world. This interconnectedness has certainly brought numerous advantages including economic opportunities and the exchange of knowledge among people. Besides, challenges like increased vulnerability to global crisis and perspectives about national statecraft have been presented, too. Moving forward, it is crucial for countries to collaborate to strike a balance between reaping the benefits of a globalized world addressing the challenges it brings making the most of the opportunities while mitigating the probable risks.

CHAPTER 1
DIPLOMACY AND INTERNATIONAL COOPERATION

THE IMPORTANCE OF DIPLOMACY IN INTERNATIONAL RELATIONS AND RESOLVING CONFLICTS

International relations and conflicts among nations have been an intrinsic part of human civilization since the time immemorial. In navigating these complex dynamics, diplomacy has emerged as an indispensible tool for managing relationships, resolving conflicts, and promoting peace and cooperation among nations. Diplomacy and international cooperation are intertwined elements in the contemporary global landscape.

While diplomacy focuses on practicing the art of negotiation and dialogue between nations, it also emphasizes collaborative efforts among countries to address shared challenges and achieve common goals. Highlighting the significance in promoting peace and advancing global progress between diplomacy and international cooperation is a crucial interplay.

Diplomacy is the art and science of maintaining peaceful relationships between nations, groups, or individuals. Often, diplomacy refers to representatives of different groups discussing such issues as conflict, trade, the environment, technology, or security.

People who practice diplomacy are called diplomats. Diplomats try to help their own country, encourage cooperation between nations, and maintain peace. A group of diplomats representing one country that lives in another country is called a diplomatic mission. A permanent diplomatic mission is called an embassy. An ambassador is the lead diplomat at an embassy. A large diplomatic mission may have representation besides a single embassy. Other places of representation are called consulates.

For example, the embassy of the United Kingdom is in the U.S. capital, Washington, D.C. The United Kingdom also has consulates in the U.S. cities of Atlanta, Georgia; Boston, Massachusetts; Chicago, Illinois; Denver, Colorado; Houston, Texas; Los Angeles, California; Miami, Florida; New York City, New York; Orlando, Florida; and San Francisco, California. The British ambassador and the rest of the British diplomatic mission are responsible for representing British policies to the U.S. government, as well as assisting British people in the U.S. This often involves helping them with legal matters, such as visas or work permits.

American diplomats work for a branch of the Department of State called the Foreign Service. More than 12,000 people work for the Foreign Service, helping Americans who travel abroad and pursuing American foreign policy. The U.S. has 265 diplomatic missions around the world. The largest U.S. diplomatic mission is in Mexico, which has an embassy in Mexico City and 22 consulates and consular agencies throughout the country.

As a matter of fact, American diplomatic missions are staffed by Foreign Service officers and Foreign Service specialists. Foreign Service officers are formal members of the Foreign Service. There are five major branches of work for Foreign Service officers: consular affairs (helping Americans living or visiting foreign countries); economic affairs; management affairs; political affairs; and public diplomacy. Public diplomacy is the practice of representing the U.S. in social and cultural activities, such as sports events, films, books, and radio broadcasts.

Foreign Service specialists provide important support services for diplomatic missions. This includes health care, construction and engineering, and English-language programs, and often Foreign Service specialists must provide security for Americans in the event of a natural disaster or political unrest in a country.

On managing international relations diplomacy plays a pivotal role in maintaining peaceful coexistence among nations. It acts as a channel for dialogue and negotiation, providing an essential opportunity for nations to address their concerns, grievances, and differences constructively. By promoting dialogue over confrontation, diplomacy helps reduce tensions, creating an environment where conflicts can be resolved through peaceful means. Furthermore it provides a framework for parties involved to come together and seek mutually acceptable solutions through negotiations and compromise.

Diplomats act as intermediaries, facilitating dialogue, and assisting in finding a common ground. International cooperation complements diplomacy by supporting conflict resolution efforts through support systems, mediation, and peacekeeping operations. Together, they contribute to the de-escalation of hostilities and the establishment of lasting peace. Different groups of people often come into conflict when a problem cannot be solved, when values clash, or when there is ambiguity over ownership of land resources. Diplomacy, the art of maintaining peaceful relationships without the use of violence, can help turn conflict into cooperation. Such diplomatic efforts foster mutual understanding, trust, and empathy, reducing the likelihood of conflicts and promoting long-term stability. Through diplomatic channels and meetings, diplomats work to understand each other's perspectives, articulate their own interests, and negotiate mutually beneficial agreements, treaties, and resolutions.

Diplomacy facilitates multilateral cooperation between countries through international organizations, treaties and agreements. Diplomats engage in diplomatic conferences and meetings, where countries collaborate on issues of global concern, negotiate trade agreements, and develop international norms and standards. These collective efforts help create a framework for addressing global challenges and advancing regional or global stability.

Regular diplomatic exchanges promote mutual respect, understanding and recognition of shared interests. Through joint projects, agreements and partnerships, countries collaborate towards achieving common objectives enhancing economic development, scientific advancements, and cultural exchange. These cooperative efforts not only strengthen bilateral relations but also contribute to a more interconnected and interdependent world.

THE ROLE OF INTERNATIONAL ORGANIZATIONS IN FACILITATING COOPERATION AMONG NATIONS

Diplomacy and international cooperation contribute to the establishment and strengthening of global governance structures. International organizations enable the countries to work together on shared challenges, resolve conflicts, and promote global development and security. International organizations establish global standards, norms, and regulations in various areas such as trade, labor, human rights, health, and environment.

They provide mediation and negotiation services, peacekeeping missions, and platforms for diplomatic dialogue to prevent and resolve conflicts among nations. Facilitating multilateral agreements and treaties: International organizations support countries in negotiating and implementing multilateral agreements and treaties. For example, the Paris Agreement on climate change was facilitated by the United Nations Framework Convention on Climate Change (UNFCCC), which brought nations together to address the global challenge of climate change.

Furthermore, International organizations play a vital role in coordinating global responses to global challenges such as pandemics, terrorism, and nuclear proliferation. They provide platforms for countries to share information, coordinate strategies, and jointly tackle these challenges.

International organizations such as the United Nations (UN), the United Nations Children's Fund (UNICEF), and the United Nations Educational, Scientific and Cultural Organization (UNESCO) have been instrumental in promoting and facilitating cooperation among nations. Through their diverse range of activities and initiatives, these organizations aim to foster dialogue, collaboration, and the establishment of common goals among member states.

They certainly aim to explore the multifaceted roles of these international organizations in facilitating cooperation among nations, including their contributions to diplomacy, conflict resolution, addressing global challenges, advocating for human rights, and promoting sustainable development.

International organizations like the UN play a crucial role in facilitating diplomacy and peace building efforts among nations. The UN serves as a platform for member states to engage in dialogue and negotiations, with the goal of resolving conflicts and promoting stability. The General Assembly and Security Council act as forums for diplomatic discussions, allowing nations to express their concerns, exchange ideas, and seek common ground.

The UN's involvement in conflict resolution extends beyond dialogue and negotiations. The organization also deploys peacekeeping missions to areas experiencing conflict, providing stability and facilitating political transitions. Peacekeepers work on the ground, promoting ceasefire agreements, protecting civilians, and facilitating the delivery of humanitarian aid. Notable examples include peacekeeping missions in Cyprus, the Democratic Republic of Congo, and South Sudan.

Furthermore, the UN focuses on brokering peace agreements and facilitating post-conflict reconstruction. The involvement of the organization in peace processes and transitional justice mechanisms helps ensure the implementation of durable solutions, promoting cooperation among nations involved in the conflicts.

International organizations serve as platforms for addressing global challenges that require cross-border cooperation. They provide spaces for nations to collaborate, share knowledge, and develop strategies to tackle shared threats and issues. Key global challenges include climate change, poverty eradication, public health crises, and sustainable development.

The UN plays a central role in addressing climate change through the United Nations Framework Convention on Climate Change (UNFCCC) and the Paris Agreement. The UNFCCC brings countries together to negotiate and discuss global responses to climate change. The Paris Agreement, under the auspices of the UNFCCC, aims to limit global warming to well below 2 degrees Celsius and provides a framework for countries to work together towards this goal.

The agreement facilitates international cooperation by encouraging countries to set their own emission reduction targets and promoting financial and technological support for developing nations.

Sustainable development is another crucial area in which international organizations play a fundamental role. The UN's Sustainable Development Goals (SDGs) provide a global framework for addressing poverty, inequality, environmental degradation, and social injustices. By promoting cooperation among nations, the SDGs assist in fostering sustainable development through initiatives such as poverty eradication, ensuring access to education, promoting gender equality, and supporting clean energy production.

During times of public health crises, international organizations like the World Health Organization (WHO) serve as key facilitators of cooperation. The WHO acts as a global platform for coordination, providing technical assistance, disseminating information, and sharing best practices. The COVID-19 pandemic highlighted the importance of international cooperation in addressing health emergencies, demonstrating the need for collaboration in areas such as research, vaccine distribution, and coordinated response efforts.

International organizations are crucial advocates for human rights, working to fight against discrimination, inequality, and human rights abuses. The UN, through bodies such as the Human Rights Council and the Office of the High Commissioner for Human Rights (OHCHR), promotes and protects human rights globally.

The Universal Declaration of Human Rights, adopted by the UN General Assembly in 1948, serves as a benchmark for human rights standards. International organizations support nation-states in implementing human rights conventions, providing technical assistance, and monitoring mechanisms to ensure compliance. Through periodic reviews, they assess member states' adherence to human rights principles and offer recommendations for improvement.

UNICEF, a specialized agency of the UN, advocates for the rights and well-being of children worldwide. Through its partnerships with governments, civil society organizations, and other stakeholders, UNICEF works to protect children's rights, provide access to education and healthcare, and address issues such as child labor and child trafficking. By promoting cooperation among nations, UNICEF helps address common challenges related to child rights and well-being.

Advocacy for human rights extends to promoting gender equality and empowering women. International organizations, including UN Women and UNESCO, work towards the elimination of gender-based discrimination and violence, and the promotion of women's participation in decision-making processes. Through various initiatives and programs, they promote cooperation among nations to address gender inequality and ensure equal rights and opportunities for all.

International organizations play a vital role in fostering global sustainable development by promoting collaboration and providing support to nations. They offer technical expertise, resources, and capacity-building support to help countries implement development projects and policies.

UNESCO is an international organization that focuses on promoting education, science, culture, and communication worldwide. Through its diverse range of programs, UNESCO helps member states develop inclusive and sustainable societies. It advocates for quality education for all, the preservation of cultural heritage, the advancement of scientific knowledge, and the promotion of freedom of expression and media development.

The UN, through its economic and social commissions and specialized agencies, supports member states in formulating and implementing global development agendas. The United Nations Development Programme (UNDP) works closely with governments to eradicate poverty, enhance governance systems, and ensure sustainable development. It provides technical assistance, shares best practices, and mobilizes resources to address development challenges and promote cooperation among nations.

In addition to the UN, international financial institutions like the World Bank play a significant role in promoting sustainable development. The World Bank supports member countries in financing and implementing development projects in areas such as infrastructure, education, healthcare, and agriculture. By collaborating with nations, providing financial resources, and leveraging global partnerships, these institutions foster cooperation and contribute to sustainable development efforts.

In conclusion, international organizations such as the UN, UNICEF, and UNESCO play crucial roles in facilitating cooperation among nations through various means. They provide platforms for diplomacy and conflict resolution, addressing global challenges, advocating for human rights, and promoting sustainable development

. By fostering dialogue, consensus-building, and coordinated action, these organizations contribute to the development, peace, and well-being of nations worldwide. In an increasingly interconnected world, the need for international cooperation has become more evident than ever before. As countries face shared challenges and pursue common goals, international organizations continue to play vital roles in facilitating cooperation and fostering a more inclusive, prosperous, and sustainable future for all.

CHAPTER 2

GLOBAL CHALLENGES AND CRISES

GLOBAL CHALLENGES OCCURING IN THE 21ST CENTURY

Global Challenges and crises refer to the complex issues that affect countries and regions across the world, often requiring collective action and cooperation to address. These challenges can have far reaching consequences and impact multiple aspects of society, including politics, economics, the environment, and human well-being.

International cooperation is crucial in tackling complex global challenges that transcend national boundaries. Collaborative and collective decision-making is required to ameliorate the issues on climate change, poverty, transnational crime, and pandemics.

The 21st century has witnessed numerous challenges that have had a profound impact on international relations. These global challenges transcend national boundaries and demand collective efforts and cooperation to find effective and sustainable solutions.

One of the most pressing global challenges in the 21st century is climate change. The increasing global temperatures, extreme weather events, and rising sea levels pose significant risks to ecosystems, economies, and human well-being. The ramifications of climate change are far-reaching and have direct implications for international relations. Nations must collaborate to reduce greenhouse gas emissions, promote sustainable practices, and adapt to the changing climate. The Paris Agreement is a testament to international cooperation to tackle climate change, where countries have committed to limiting global warming and promoting sustainable development.

Additionally, the outbreak and spread of infectious diseases have showcased the interconnectedness of the global community. Illnesses such as Ebola, Zika, and most recently, the COVID-19 pandemic, have had severe impacts on public health, economies, and political stability. These pandemics have underscored the need for international collaboration in surveillance, preparedness, and response efforts.

They have also exposed the vulnerabilities and limitations of existing global health systems. Countries must work together to strengthen health infrastructure, share information and resources, develop vaccines, and improve global pandemic preparedness.

While terrorism remains a significant challenge to global security in the 21st century, transnational extremist networks are destabilizing regions and carrying out attacks worldwide. The fight against terrorism requires international cooperation in intelligence sharing, counter-terrorism measures, and efforts to counter the ideologies that breed extremism. Effective coordination and collaboration among nations are essential to tackle the root causes of terrorism, disrupt terrorist financing networks, and promote peace and stability.

Furthermore, the displacement of people due to conflicts, persecution, and economic factors has resulted in a significant refugee and migration crisis around the world. This mass movement of people imposes social, economic, and political challenges on both the host nations and the migrants themselves. It requires international cooperation to manage and address these crises effectively. Nations must work together to provide humanitarian aid, address the root causes of displacement, and develop comprehensive and humane migration policies.

The proliferation of nuclear weapons and the potential for their use poses grave threats to international security. Preventing the spread of nuclear weapons requires concerted diplomatic efforts, non-proliferation agreements, and disarmament initiatives. The Treaty on the Non-Proliferation of Nuclear Weapons (NPT) aims to curb the proliferation of nuclear weapons and promote disarmament. However, the challenges of non-compliance, nuclear threats from rogue states, and the emergence of new nuclear powers necessitate constant engagement and cooperation among nations in nuclear security and disarmament efforts.

Economic inequality, both within and between nations, poses significant social, political, and economic challenges in the 21st century. The increasing gap between the rich and the poor exacerbates social unrest, threatens political stability, and hampers sustainable development.

Addressing economic inequality requires international cooperation to promote inclusive economic growth, fair trade practices, and policies that reduce poverty and improve livelihoods. The United Nations' Sustainable Development

Goals (SDGs) emphasize the need for cooperation among nations to eradicate poverty, reduce inequality, and achieve inclusive and sustainable development.

The digital age has brought about new challenges to global security in the form of cyber threats. Hacking, data breaches, and cyber-attacks pose a significant risk to national and international security, as they can disrupt critical infrastructure, steal sensitive information, and compromise individuals' privacy. The interconnectedness of digital networks demands international cooperation in establishing norms, rules, and regulations to address cyber threats effectively. Collaboration among nations is crucial in sharing information, developing cybersecurity capabilities, and combating cybercrime.

The challenges faced in the 21st century have highlighted the interdependence of nations and the need for international cooperation. Climate change, global health pandemics, terrorism, refugee crises, nuclear proliferation, economic inequality, and cybersecurity all require collective efforts and diplomatic collaboration.

The success of addressing these global challenges lies in the willingness of nations to set aside their differences and work harmoniously towards shared goals. International relations in the 21st century must focus on promoting dialogue, fostering cooperation, and finding sustainable solutions to these challenges, ensuring a secure, prosperous, and sustainable future for all.

In addressing these interconnected challenges, international organizations such as the United Nations, World Health Organization, and World Trade Organization play vital roles in facilitating collaboration among nations. These forums provide platforms for dialogue, negotiation, and the formulation of shared policies and strategies.

Effective collaboration among nations requires a commitment to multilateralism, mutual respect, and the recognition of shared interests. It also demands the acknowledgment that no nation can tackle these challenges in isolation. By fostering a culture of collaboration, nations can pool resources, expertise, and perspectives to develop innovative solutions, promote peace and stability, and build a more prosperous and sustainable future for all.

Only through collective efforts, shared knowledge, and coordinated actions can we effectively address these challenges. By working together, nations can forge a path towards a more resilient, inclusive, and sustainable world for present and future generations.

CHAPTER 3
ECONOMIC GLOBALIZATION AND TRADE

INFLUENCE OF GLOBAL TRADE IN INTERNATIONAL RELATIONS

Global trade, often referred to as international trade, is a fundamental aspect of the global economy. It entails the exchange of goods, services, and capital across international borders, contributing to economic growth and development worldwide. Global trade involves the buying and selling of goods and services between nations, as well as international investment flows.

The concept of global trade is based on the principle of comparative advantage, which suggests that countries should focus on producing and exporting goods and services in which they have a comparative advantage, while importing goods and services in which other countries excel. This allows for the optimal allocation of resources, promoting efficiency and specialization on a global scale.

International trade is facilitated through various channels, including trade agreements, tariff barriers, and global institutions such as the World Trade Organization (WTO). Trade agreements, such as free trade agreements and customs unions, aim to reduce tariffs and other trade barriers among participating countries, fostering conditions for increased trade flows. Tariff barriers, such as import duties and quotas, are imposed to protect domestic industries or regulate imports, but can also restrict global trade.

Global trade has numerous benefits for participating countries. It enables access to a wider range of goods and services, allowing consumers to benefit from enhanced quality, variety, and competitive prices. Additionally, global trade promotes economic growth by stimulating business competitiveness, innovation, and productivity. It offers opportunities for countries to specialize in their comparative advantages, leading to increased output and efficiency gains. Furthermore, trade can contribute to poverty alleviation by creating employment opportunities and driving economic development.

However, global trade also introduces challenges and concerns. It can result in trade imbalances, where some nations consistently export more than they import, leading to economic inequality and potential social and political tensions. Trade disputes may arise when countries impose unfair trade practices, such as dumping or subsidizing domestic industries, harming their competitors. Moreover, global trade can impact the environment through increased carbon emissions and resource use, necessitating sustainable trade practices.

Global trade plays a crucial role in shaping the modern global economy. It facilitates the exchange of goods, services, and capital between countries, promoting economic growth, development, and specialization. While it brings numerous benefits, challenges and concerns also arise, necessitating careful management and regulation to ensure a fair and sustainable global trading system.

Global trade has become increasingly interconnected with international relations, and its influence has had far-reaching impacts on various aspects of the global political economy. This article will explore the influence of global trade in international relations, focusing on the economic, political, and social dimensions.

Economically, global trade has transformed the world into an interconnected marketplace, enabling countries to exchange goods and services across borders. This has led to increased economic interdependence among nations, with each country relying on others for resources, technologies, and markets. The expansion of global trade has resulted in the growth of multinational corporations, supply chains, and global value chains, creating a global division of labor. As a result, countries are increasingly compelled to consider the economic implications of their foreign policies and to actively engage in trade negotiations and agreements to enhance their economic competitiveness.

The influence of global trade on international politics cannot be underestimated. Trade has become a powerful tool for states to pursue their national interests and project their power on the global stage. This is evident in the rise of economic diplomacy, where states use trade negotiations and agreements to advance their political goals. For example, countries may use trade sanctions or tariffs to pressure other nations to change their behavior or comply with specific demands. Furthermore, global trade has altered the balance of power among states, as economic strength is now a significant determinant of a country's overall influence in international relations. Countries with strong economies are often better positioned to shape global norms and institutions to reflect their interests.

The social dimension of global trade has also had a profound influence on international relations. Trade has not only facilitated the exchange of goods and services but has also led to the transfer of ideas, cultures, and people across borders. This has resulted in the blending of cultures and the creation of multicultural societies in many countries. In addition, global trade has brought about social and cultural changes within societies, such as increased consumerism, the spread of Western values, and the erosion of traditional livelihoods. These social changes can spark tensions and conflicts both within and between nations, as societies grapple with the challenges of globalization and its impact on their social fabric.

While global trade has undeniable benefits, it also gives rise to various challenges and dilemmas in international relations. One major challenge is the issue of economic inequality, both within and between countries. The benefits of global trade are not evenly distributed, with some countries and individuals benefiting more than others. This disparity can lead to social and political unrest, exacerbating existing tensions and creating new fault lines in international relations. Furthermore, global trade can have negative environmental consequences, such as increased carbon emissions and depletion of natural resources, which can strain international relations and cooperation on environmental issues.

The influence of global trade in international relations is multi-dimensional. It has transformed the world into an interconnected marketplace, expanded economic interdependence, and reshaped power dynamics among nations. Global trade has also become a powerful tool for states to pursue their interests and project their power. However, it also presents various challenges, including economic inequality and environmental degradation. As global trade continues to evolve, its influence on international relations will continue to shape the global political economy.

HOW WORLD TRADE ORGANIZATION IS INTERCONNECTING THE COUNTRIES

The World Trade Organization (WTO) plays a crucial role in connecting countries across the globe through various mechanisms. Established in 1995, the WTO is an international organization that deals with the global rules of trade between nations. Its primary objective is to ensure that trade flows as smoothly, predictably, and freely as possible.

One of the key ways in which the WTO connects countries is by promoting and enforcing international trade agreements. The organization oversees the implementation and enforcement of the General Agreement on Tariffs and Trade (GATT) and its successor, the Agreement on Trade-Related Aspects of Intellectual Property Rights (TRIPS). These agreements provide a framework for countries to negotiate and resolve trade disputes, fostering transparency and stability in international trade.

Moreover, the WTO facilitates negotiations among member countries to liberalize trade by reducing barriers such as tariffs and quotas. Through rounds of negotiations, countries come together to discuss and reach agreements on issues ranging from agricultural subsidies to intellectual property rights. These negotiations not only have implications for trade flows but also provide a platform for countries to engage in dialogue and deepen their economic ties.

Another way in which the WTO connects countries is by providing a platform for capacity building and technical assistance. The organization assists developing nations in understanding and complying with trade rules, thus helping them integrate into the global trading system. The WTO's Aid for Trade initiative aims to enhance the ability of developing countries to trade by providing financial and technical assistance to address trade-related infrastructure gaps and build institutional capacity. By connecting countries through capacity building, the WTO contributes to reducing the economic disparities between nations and promoting inclusive growth.

Furthermore, the WTO acts as a forum for dispute settlement between countries. It provides a framework for resolving trade conflicts through a rules-based system. When disputes arise, member countries can bring their cases to the WTO's Dispute Settlement Body, which consists of independent panels authorized to make rulings on trade disputes. This mechanism encourages countries to engage in negotiations and find mutually beneficial solutions, minimizing the chances of trade conflicts escalating into full-blown trade wars. By resolving disputes in a fair and impartial manner, the WTO strengthens the trust and cooperation between countries.

The WTO also connects countries by serving as a platform for information sharing and cooperation. Through its Trade Policy Review Mechanism, each member country's trade policies and practices are subject to peer review. This process provides an opportunity for countries to learn from each other's experiences, share best practices, and identify areas where improvements can be made. By fostering transparency and dialogue, the WTO helps build trust among countries and promotes convergence towards common trade principles and practices.

In conclusion, the World Trade Organization plays a critical role in connecting countries in today's globalized world. Through promoting and enforcing international trade agreements, facilitating negotiations, providing technical assistance, resolving disputes, and serving as a platform for information sharing and cooperation, the WTO promotes trade connectivity among nations. By doing so, the organization supports economic growth, reduces inequalities, and fosters mutual understanding and cooperation between countries.

WORLD-TRADE ORGANIZATIONS SUCH AS AMAZON AND ALIBABA

In today's increasingly interconnected world, global trade has become an essential driver of economic growth and development. The rise of e-commerce giants like Amazon and Alibaba has significantly influenced the interconnectedness of nations worldwide. This part of the book aims to analyze and discuss the impactful role played by Amazon and Alibaba as world trade organizations, focusing on their influence in fostering economic interconnectedness, technological advancements, and the challenges and opportunities they present.

Economic Interconnectedness

Amazon and Alibaba have revolutionized the global marketplace, connecting buyers and sellers from different corners of the world. Both companies provide digital platforms that facilitate the exchange of a wide range of goods and services, transcending national boundaries. By leveraging their vast networks, logistics capabilities, and market reach, Amazon and Alibaba have enabled small and medium-sized enterprises (SMEs) to expand their customer base globally. This economic interconnectedness enables SMEs to overcome traditional trade barriers, reducing costs and expanding market opportunities. Furthermore, these platforms foster entrepreneurship and innovation by allowing individuals to establish and operate businesses with minimal physical infrastructure.

CHAPTER 4
EMERGING OPPORTUNITIES

Technological Advancements

The success of Amazon and Alibaba can be attributed to their relentless pursuit of technological advancements. Both companies have continually invested in cutting-edge technologies, including artificial intelligence, machine learning, and big data analytics. These advancements have revolutionized the efficiency of supply chain management, customer analytics, personalized recommendations, and logistics operations. The availability of these technologies has enabled businesses, particularly SMEs, to adopt modern business practices, optimize operations, and enhance productivity. Moreover, Amazon and Alibaba's technological expertise has spurred innovation and competitiveness among other businesses, thus fostering an interconnected network of companies striving to remain competitive in the digital era.

Challenges and Opportunities

While the influence of Amazon and Alibaba on global interconnectedness is largely positive, it also raises certain challenges and opportunities. For instance, the dominance of these e-commerce giants has led to concerns over the concentration of economic power. Their ability to gather vast amounts of customer data raises privacy concerns and prompts debates about data protection policies. Additionally, the disruption caused by these platforms has posed challenges to traditional brick-and-mortar businesses. Nevertheless, the rise of platforms like Amazon and Alibaba has created new opportunities for employment, entrepreneurship, and cross-border trade. By tapping into these platforms, small businesses can access global markets, diversify revenue streams, and harness the power of digital technologies.

In conclusion, Amazon and Alibaba have become significant world trade organizations that have profoundly influenced the interconnectedness of nations. By fostering economic interconnectedness, driving technological advancements, and creating opportunities amidst challenges, these e-commerce giants play a pivotal role in shaping the global marketplace and transforming traditional business models.

www.ingramcontent.com/pod-product-compliance
Lightning Source LLC
LaVergne TN
LVHW010421070526
838199LV00064B/5370